Hairy, scary, Ordinary

What is an Adjective?

Hairy, scary, Ordinary

What is an Adjective?

by Brian P. Cleary

illustrated by Jenya Prosmitsky

BOOK HOUSE

Adjectives are words like hairy

scary,

cool and ordinary.

They tell us
things are

orange
or
green,

Hot or cold
or in-between,

Leaky, squeaky, ancient, new,

easy, breezy, broken, blue.

Adjectives help to tell us more,

Like narrow street or favourite store,

Hilly, chilly, fast and fun,

Undercooked and overdone.

They tell us
of an old
black boot,

A rainy day,
a wrinkled
suit,

A silly teacher, giant hair,

A big fat cow at the local fair -

Footballs that are red and rubber,

Spot's clean fur each time you scrub her,

Cold dark
mornings,
sunny
weather,
sipping ice-cold
drinks
together.

That treats are yummy,

shakes are thick,

And if you're feeling well or sick.

They're colourful, like mauve and puce,

They help explain, like lean and loose,

Adjectives are words like flashy.

Vibrant, bright, and somewhat trashy,

Frilly,
silly,

polka-dotted,

single-looped

or

double-knotted.

They modify **nouns**
in ways that tell us

if
someone's
sincere,

delighted, or jealous,

If jackets are  herringbone,

plaid,

or stripy,

If babies are

happy,

contented or gripey.

They tell us
that
TV
is

funny or bad,

Of books that
are stuffy,
amazing, or sad,

Adjectives help us describe when we're weary,

Or say when we're grumpy

or when we are cheery.

Without 'em we couldn't tell Mum how we feel,

Like hungry, or hurting, or ready to squeal.

Lopsided, one-sided
ball games that bore us,

The sweet gentle sounds
that descend from the chorus,

Mighty blue oceans and tiny red rings,

Adjectives tell us all of these things.

So, what is an

adjective?

Do you know?

AUTHOR: BRIAN P. CLEARY is the author of several other books for children, including *To root, to toot, to parachute: What is a Verb?*

ILLUSTRATOR: JENYA PROSMITSKY grew up and studied art in Kishinev, Moldova, and now lives in Minneapolis in the USA. Her two cats, Henry and Freddy, were vital to her illustrations for this book.

Published in Great Britain in 2003 by
Book House, an imprint of
The Salariya Book Company Ltd
25 Marlborough Place, Brighton BN1 1UB

Please visit the Salariya Book Company at:
www.salariya.com
www.book-house.co.uk

ISBN 1 904194 58 3

A catalogue record for this book is available from the British Library.

Printed and bound in USA.